MICHELANGELO

MICHELANGELO

Genius of the
Renaissance
by Jayne Pettit

A Book Report Biography
FRANKLIN WATTS
A Division of Grolier Publishing
New York / London / Hong Kong / Sydney
Danbury, Connecticut

Photographs ©: Art Resource: 3, 9, 19, 25, 27, 31, 34, 43, 44, 46, 49, 53, 54, 58, 70, 76, 78, 81, 83, 94, 99, 110, 114, 116; Bridgeman Art Library Int'l Ltd., London/New York: cover, 12, 20, 85, 89, 96; Corbis-Bettmann: 2, 18, 101.

Visit Franklin Watts on the Internet at:
http://publishing.grolier.com

Library of Congress Cataloging-in-Publication Data

Michelangelo / Jayne Pettit.
      p. cm.—(A book report biography)
    Includes bibliographical references and index.
    Summary: Recounts the life of the famous sculptor, painter, poet, and architect who flourished during the Italian Renaissance.
    ISBN 0-531-11490-2
    1. Michelangelo Buonarroti, 1475–1564. 2. Artists—Italy—Biography. [1. Michelangelo Buonarroti, 1475–1564. 2. Artists.] I. Title. II. Series.
    N6923.B9P45 1998
    709'.2-dc21
    [B]   98-26724
                                           CIP
                                         AC

CONTENTS

This book is dedicated with love to my
history and literature students at
Hilton Head Preparatory School
Hilton Head, South Carolina

DARE TO DREAM!

Good painting is nothing else but a
copy of the perfections of God and
a reminder of His painting.
—Michelangelo Buonarroti

CHAPTER 1

GENIUS OF THE RENAISSANCE

On November 2, 1512, the massive doors to the Sistine Chapel in Rome were thrown open to a host of papal dignitaries who had gathered for a long-awaited occasion, the unveiling of Michelangelo's magnificent painting of scenes from the Old Testament. They were stunned by what they saw. Craning their necks, they gazed in wonder at the vaulted ceiling 80 feet (24 meters) above their heads. Before their eyes, a beautiful *fresco* bursting with life and energy played out the biblical story of the dawning of the world. Stretching 5,800 square feet across the length and breadth of the room and containing more than 300 figures, the fresco marked the completion of a project that had been more than four years in the making.

Less than a week before, frightened by the last of Pope Julius II's tirades and threats against him, Michelangelo had ordered the scaffolding upon which he had worked removed. He was exhausted, his body racked with pain and his vision blurred by years of agonizing toil in self-imposed solitude. Frustrated and plagued by fears of death that tormented him throughout his life, he once described his feelings in a sonnet to a friend:

> My beard toward heaven, I feel the back of
>   my brain
> Upon my neck, I grow the breast of a Harpy;*
> My brush, above my face continually,
> Makes it a splendid floor by dripping down . . .
> I'm not in a good place, and I'm no painter.

By age 37, Michelangelo had already created his powerful sculptures of the *Pietà* and the monumental *David*. Twenty-nine years later, his final fresco for the Sistine Chapel, the *Last Judgment*, would bring both praise and criticism. During the intervening years, he would continue his work under a succession of popes, dividing his time between Rome and his beloved Florence. He would spend the last 17 of his 89 years on earth as the architect of St. Peter's Basilica in Rome. Dur-

---

*Harpy—in Greek mythology, a winged beast with a woman's head and body.

ing his lifetime, he would write more than 300 poems, including 80 sonnets (his favorite form of poetry), and 100 madrigals, many of which were scribbled on drawings and sketches. Some modern scholars have called him the greatest Italian lyric poet of the sixteenth century.

Stubborn and frequently ill-tempered, yet kind and affectionate toward those he trusted, Michelangelo was the genius of the *Renaissance* and the creator of some of the world's most remarkable works of art.

CHAPTER 2

THE YOUNG APPRENTICE

The little hill town of Caprese, Italy, has witnessed few changes during the past five hundred years. Located several miles southeast of Florence and tucked into a rugged, mountainous landscape dotted by grazing sheep, olive trees, and vineyards, it is home to fewer than 3,000 people, many of whom are descendants of ancient tribes who once inhabited this lovely region which we call Tuscany today.

In the autumn of 1474, Lodovico di Buonarroti Simoni, the newly appointed magistrate of Caprese, arrived in Tuscany with his pregnant wife Francesca and infant son Lionardo. He began a six-month term as *podestà*, or chief magistrate, of Caprese and the neighboring village of Chiusi. Along the way, Francesca had suffered a fall from her horse, and Lodovico feared that she might lose her child.

Despite her frail condition, however, Francesca recovered from her injuries and on March 6, 1475, gave birth to a son. A short time afterward, the little one was baptized in the local chapel. His father named him Michelangelo.

Six weeks later, Lodovico's term as *podestà* ended, and the Buonarroti family returned to Florence. Michelangelo's 19-year-old mother, a sickly woman about whom little is known, found that she could no longer nurse her son. She turned the baby over to the wife of a stonecutter in the nearby village of Settignano. Young Michelangelo became part of that family, and as he grew he absorbed the life of the hearty quarrymen of the surrounding hills. By nature strong, curious, and full of boundless energy, the child learned to handle the tools of the stonecutter, later saying, "With my nurse's milk I sucked in the hammer and chisels I use for my statues." It was to this region of stonecutters and northward to the great quarries of Carrara that the artist would repeatedly return to select blocks of gleaming white marble that would serve as the material for his magnificent sculptures.

"Giorgio, if my brains are any good at all," the artist would one day tell Giorgio Vasari, an artist friend and one of his influential biographers, "it's because I was born in the pure air of your countryside."

When Michelangelo was ten years old, his father remarried and brought Michelangelo back to Florence, placing him under the guidance of Francesco d'Urbino, a teacher of Greek and Latin. But the boy was restless and bored with his formal studies, frequently running away to sketch the new surroundings he had quickly learned to love and to watch local artists at work. Lodovico, a vain and demanding man who expected his sons to enter Florence's thriving business world, disapproved of his strong-willed offspring and often beat him severely. Despite the beatings from Lodovico and an assortment of belligerent uncles, Michelangelo continued to ignore his books and to run away from his classes.

The battles between Michelangelo and his father raged for three years, until Lodovico finally gave in to his son's protests and apprenticed him to Domenico Ghirlandaio, a prominent Florentine painter. Ghirlandaio and his brother conducted a large studio for aspiring young artists. The contract binding Michelangelo to the masters read:

I, Lodovico ... yield my son Michelangelo

1488. I, Lodovico ... yield my son Michelangelo, to Domenico and David de Tommaso di Currado for the next three years in accordance with the following terms: that the said Michelangelo must remain with the above-named masters during this time, to learn the art of painting . . . and to be at the orders of the above-named.

In the challenging environment of the Ghirlandaio studio, Michelangelo began to find himself, filling his notebooks with copies of paintings by earlier artists whom he admired—Giotto, Masaccio and other Tuscan masters. His detailed and dimensional lines demonstrated his growing fascination with the study of sculpture and the human form.

As the months passed, Michelangelo learned the techniques of painting and drawing. Francesco Granacci, a 19-year-old student in the class, took notice of the young boy's talent and encouraged him to follow his instincts. On occasions when they were not expected to be in the studio, the two traveled about the city, sketching and studying the architecture, paintings, and sculpture of the masters. Under Granacci's influence, Michelangelo nurtured his independent spirit at a point in history when Florence was intellectually and artistically the center of Renaissance learning and accomplishment. For the young student, Florence was a classroom full of wonder.

Michelangelo was blessed with an extraordinary visual memory. In his lifetime, he would sketch thousands of drawings. Ascanio Condivi, who would one day become a close friend and a biographer, wrote, "I heard him say that he never drew a line which he didn't remember." Condivi claimed that Michelangelo never repeated his own artwork because *"he remembered everything that he had done."* And if that weren't enough, he could also produce a perfect replica of another artist's work after having seen it only once!

"He never drew a line which he didn't remember."

As an apprentice in the Ghirlandaio workshop, Michelangelo soon demonstrated to his master that he was no ordinary student. On one occasion, a number of the students were working on a fresco project for one of Ghirlandaio's most important commissions, the church of Santa Maria Novella. One day, the master left the studio after having given each apprentice his assignment. Michelangelo busied himself at his desk, glancing up from time to time to watch a number of students up on a scaffolding who were involved with the fresco. Curious about the action taking place, he began to sketch different members of the group. Ghirlandaio returned to the studio as Michelangelo completed his drawing, took one look at it and was so "amazed at the power and originality of the lad's work that he exclaimed, 'This boy knows more than I do.'"

"This boy knows more than I do."

During the summer of 1489, Lorenzo de Medici, of Florence's great Medici family, was organizing a school of sculpture on the grounds of the San Marco gardens, his private park near a monastery of the same name. A brilliant intellectual and patron of literature and the arts, Lorenzo had amassed an enviable collection of ancient sculptures for his park. He was eager to encourage young artists to become sculptors since Florentine interest in sculpture had come to a virtual standstill.

Lorenzo believed that the San Marco gardens would inspire the students of his new school. With the location settled, he asked Domenico Ghirlandaio to assist him in selecting talented young students. Among those suggested were Michelangelo Buonarroti and Francesco Granacci.

Later that summer, 14-year-old Michelangelo entered the San Marco gardens to begin the most important phase of his development as an artist. This period would have a lasting effect upon him and profoundly influence his intellectual, spiritual, and artistic growth throughout a lifetime of incredible achievement.

*Lorenzo de Medici noticed the young
Michelangelo's genius.*

CHAPTER 3

MOVING IN WITH THE MEDICIS

The world that Michelangelo entered during that summer of 1489 was alive with the spirit, brilliance, and energy of the Renaissance, a time in history that witnessed a revival of ancient learning. This flowering of intellectual, scientific, and artistic achievement was unparalleled since the glorious days of the Roman Empire.

The city that became the seed from which the Renaissance grew and flourished began as part of an important trade route between northern and southern Europe. In Florence and its surrounding territories, trade encouraged the growth of ideas, initiative, and a spirit of individualism. In time, the area became the center of a thriving textile and manufacturing industry, importing precious silks, woolens, and other materials from abroad. Inspired by the continuing expansion of trade, Florentine moneylenders became bankers to

*When Michelangelo was growing up, Florence was a
city bursting with the energy of the Renaissance.*

European royalty and served as the financial
agents of the Roman Catholic Church. Florence
had established itself as the monetary capital of
Europe.

The spread of industry and wealth allowed
several rich men to patronize artists and their
creations. The household into which the young
Michelangelo was introduced had its beginnings
almost a century before when Giovanni de Medici,
the great-grandfather of Lorenzo, amassed a for-
tune as a banker. Giovanni's son, Cosimo, expanded the family's banking fortunes and became
heavily involved in politics. He worked behind the
scenes and manipulated the affairs of the Repub-

lic, as the city-state of Florence was called. Cosimo's grandson, Lorenzo, had similar ideas. "In Florence," he once said, "it is difficult for a man to remain wealthy unless he has the upper hand in politics."

But business and politics are not the keys to a man's soul. Educated by Renaissance humanists, Lorenzo developed a love of learning and self-expression. While managing four country estates along with his Florentine palace, planting botanical gardens, and devoting time to charitable causes, Lorenzo gave generous support to artists in many fields. A fine musician and composer, as well as a poet of distinction, the man Florentines affectionately called Lorenzo the Magnificent found great joy in all aspects of life. He gathered together under his roof the leading artists, poets, and scholars of his day. Many of them found permanent living quarters in the spacious palace that had become known as the "hotel of princes."

This was the atmosphere into which Lorenzo de Medici welcomed the young Michelangelo that summer day in 1489. Imagine the awe with which the boy must have greeted his surroundings—the graciousness of the palace, the dazzling works of art, the sun-filled rooms bursting with precious books and manuscripts. To curious, gifted Michelangelo, the Medicis' world must have been staggering.

Lorenzo, acting upon Ghirlandaio's recommendation, terminated the youngster's apprenticeship and enrolled him in his new school for sculptors. According to Condivi, after Lorenzo had observed Michelangelo at work in the San Marco gardens, he took the boy aside and said, "Go, and tell your father that I wish to speak with him." Lodovico, with his customary doubts about the difference between an artist and an ignorant stonecutter, went into one of his frequent rages, insisting that Lorenzo wanted to lead his son astray.

> **"Go, and tell your father that I wish to speak with him."**

"Nevertheless," Condivi continued, "when Lodovico appeared before [Lorenzo] and was asked if he would consent to give his son up to the great man's guardianship, he did not know how to refuse. 'In faith,' the father added, 'not Michelangelo alone, but all of us, with our lives and all our abilities, are at the pleasure of your Magnificence.'"

And so Michelangelo was taken into Lorenzo's household, given clothing and an allowance, and welcomed into the Medici family. For three years, Michelangelo studied at San Marco under the skilled tutelage of Bertoldo di Giovanni, an aging sculptor and fellow houseguest at the Medici palace. Quite possibly, the precocious student also worked with another master at the gardens, an unknown but highly respected artist by the name of Benedetto da Maiano. From these fine teachers, Michelangelo's gift as a sculptor began to emerge.

Quickly recognized as a favorite of Lorenzo's, Michelangelo aroused jealousy among his fellow students. One of them, a young artist by the name of Pietro Torrigiani, got into a fight with Michelangelo at the church of Santa Maria del Carmine, where the class was sketching from a fresco. At the height of the melee, Torrigiani landed a violent punch on Michelangelo's nose, bragging later that he could feel the bones crunching beneath his fingers. The injury caused permanent damage, disfiguring Michelangelo's face and giving him the sad expression that he would wear for the rest of his life.

Other experiences as a member of the Medici family proved far more pleasant. The historian Vincent Cronin wrote, "In the most civilized household in Europe, the young genius dined at the family table, met distinguished guests, played with the children." During those memorable evenings in the spacious, candlelit dining hall, the young student was exposed to the leading scholars, poets, painters, and sculptors of his day. From these brilliant scholars, Michelangelo learned of the intellectual, religious, and moral issues debated throughout Europe.

The distinguished guests at Lorenzo's table

soon began to take notice of the precocious youngster seated with them. Condivi wrote, "All of these illustrious men paid him close attention and encouraged him in the honorable art which he had chosen." Lorenzo did so as well, sending for Michelangelo "oftentimes in a day," in order to introduce him to the magnificent works of art in the Medici collection.

For three years, possibly the happiest and most secure period of his life, Michelangelo worked and studied. One of the favorite pastimes among the guests in the Medici household was to gather together after dinner to make up light verses to the tune of Lorenzo's lute. On these occasions, young Michelangelo found himself immersed in a new form of artistic expression. Was it during these pleasurable evenings of sonnets and madrigals that he first began to think of putting his own thoughts in verse? Certainly the poems that an older Michelangelo first wrote were influenced by these early years with the Medicis.

During his hours with Bertoldo in the San Marco gardens, Michelangelo found an immediate affinity for marble, the familiar stone of his childhood in Settignano. With hammer and chisel, a young prodigy in search of himself poured his creative energies into his first attempts at sculpture.

One of them, the remarkable *Madonna of the*

Michelangelo's first masterpiece:
Madonna of the Stairs

Stairs, reveals Michelangelo's respect for the fluid style of Donatello, the greatest of the early Renaissance sculptors. What is astonishing, however, is that in this *bas-relief* (a sculpture figure or series of figures attached to a background) a boy who had not yet reached age 17 had demonstrated the techniques of a master sculptor. Vasari was so impressed that he described the work as "so exactly like Donatello's in manner that it really looks like a Donatello, *except that it is more graceful and better designed.*"

"Except that it is more graceful and better designed."

Less than a year later, the second of these reliefs, the *Battle of the Lapiths and the Centaurs*, was completed. With dramatic realism, Michelangelo's deft hand captured the terrifying movement of savage man-beasts locked in mortal combat. This early venture set the stage for the great works to come. Michelangelo was particularly fond of the *Battle of the Lapiths and the Centaurs* and kept it with him all his life.

In addition to their artistic beauty, these early sculptural works demonstrate two opposing themes that would appear, in one form or another, in much of Michelangelo's work. The first theme is dramatic movement and expression, which is cap-

In the Battle of the Lapiths and the Centaurs, *Michelangelo expressed movement and passion.*

tured by the twisting, writhing warriors in *Battle of the Lapiths and the Centaurs.* The second theme is peaceful and contemplative, exploring the silent meditations of the religious soul. This is represented in the bas-relief, *Madonna of the*

Stairs. These opposing views would appear in Michelangelo's work throughout his life.

In 1492, Michelangelo mourned the death of his patron, Lorenzo the Magnificent. But Lorenzo's death caused more than just Michelangelo's grief, it also started the decline of an era Lorenzo had helped to create. With his acute intelligence and gifts for personal diplomacy, Lorenzo had kept the warring factions of Italian politics at bay for decades. His honesty in leadership and broad range of interests had earned him the respect and confidence of the people of Florence.

Following Lorenzo's death, a grieving Michelangelo left the palace of the Medicis and the gardens of San Marco. Taking up residence in the stormy environment amidst his father, brothers and uncles, he kept to himself and his craft, working and studying alone for the next two years.

Since the days of his apprenticeship with Ghirlandaio, Michelangelo had been drawn to a study of the male human form in all of its beauty and complexity. Sketching from the works of Masaccio and Giotto, he used his pen in such a way as to suggest the structure of the body beneath the folds of a figure's garment.

But for a young genius in search of perfection, the suggestion was not enough. In order to give life and breath to the human form, he needed to learn how it worked. How did the body move?

What was the relationship between the action of bone and muscle? What role did emotion play in the action of the body? These questions could only be answered by an intensive study of human anatomy.

Michelangelo wasted no time in finding a source for his research. Through the help of an acquaintance in the city, he was allowed to transport cadavers from a local hospital to his family's home near the church of Santa Croce. Here, behind closed doors in the privacy of his studio, he acquired the knowledge he sought.

Michelangelo dissected corpses, studying firsthand the interplay between muscle, bone, and tissue. Each day brought fresh discoveries as he toiled hour after hour, sketching his findings in his notebooks. It was a grisly task, but he was driven to accomplish his goal. Condivi later wrote that the artist was forced to stop the practice "because his long handling of them [the corpses] had so affected his stomach."

The results of his determined efforts are clear. Michelangelo's mastery of the intricacies of human anatomy is apparent in every example of his art after that time. Through the years, he would continue to demand perfection of himself. And the struggle to achieve that perfection was, at times, beyond comprehension.

Between 1492 and 1494, the political situation in Florence deteriorated under the disastrous leadership of Lorenzo's son, Pietro. Young and impulsive, Pietro lacked his father's ability to govern, and tensions mounted as the city found itself without direction.

Two years after Lorenzo's death, Florence was invaded by the king of France. Pietro signed a humiliating agreement in order to restore peace. Angered by this, the citizens revolted against the Medicis, and the massive bell atop the city hall tolled in mourning for their lost republic. Pietro, with the permission of the French king, assembled his followers and quickly rode away. Michelangelo, fearful because of his close ties with the Medici family, panicked and headed for refuge in Bologna.

The glorious period of Renaissance Florence had come to an end. At its height, Marsilio Ficino had commented, "This century, like a golden age, has restored to light the liberal arts . . . poetry, rhetoric, sculpture, architecture, music . . . all this in Florence." The city would survive, but it would never again recover the brilliance of that time.

"This century, like a golden age, has restored to light the liberal arts."

CHAPTER 4

ROME, THE PIETÀ, AND THE DAVID

After a brief stay in Venice, Michelangelo arrived in Bologna during the autumn of 1494. Not long after, a noble patron of the arts took notice of his talent and invited him into his household, as was customary at that time. Soon the young man was at work, carving three marble statues to complete a tomb. These lovely figures, a kneeling angel and two saints, are among the sculptor's earliest works.

After a year in Bologna, a homesick Michelangelo returned to his beloved Florence. But the political situation in Florence deteriorated, and Michelangelo left for Rome. Arriving there in June 1496, he discovered an ancient city devastated by time. On his walks about the city, the young sculptor found the Roman Forum in ruins amid the squalor and filth of a cattle market. The once grand Colosseum had become host to a series of cheap shops and drinking taverns, and the ancient baths had become a hideout for thieves. Yet Michelangelo sensed the beauty that had once been Rome. "There are many fine things here," he wrote.

Eager for employment, he found another patron, a wealthy banker named Jacopo Galli, who ordered a statue of Bacchus, a symbol of delight and earthy pleasures. "We have bought a piece of marble for a life-size figure," Michelangelo wrote, "and I shall begin work on Monday."

Bacchus proved to be the beginning of a string of great works. A French cardinal who was a member of the Vatican's papal court employed him to carve a "Pietà of marble . . . a Virgin Mary, clothed, with the dead Christ in her arms, of the size of a proper man, for the price of 450 gold ducats of the papal mint."

"A Virgin Mary, clothed, with the dead Christ in her arms."

For years, it was the custom for many European artists to paint or carve their interpretation of the *pietà*, which is Italian for "the pity" or "the compassion." Most previous pietàs were intentionally gruesome and dark, and designed to shock the faithful with the enormity of Christ's sacrifice for them.

But Michelangelo's *Pietà* came from a dramatically different perspective. Challenging himself to concentrate on what he called "the heart's image," he took up hammer and chisel and began chipping away at the masterpiece he predicted "would equal anything past or present . . . the finest work in marble which Rome today can show."

> **"The finest work in marble which Rome today can show."**

Less than three years later, Michelangelo completed the work he had set out to achieve. In his break with the artistic conventions of the past, he discarded the concept of the finality of death and carved instead an image of a Christ whose distended veins still throbbed with the pulse of life. Here was a figure in quiet repose, a sleeping savior whose promise to the world was one of eternal life. "If life pleases us," Michelangelo wrote, "death, being made by the hands of the same creator, should not displease us."

Combining the earthly with the spiritual in the *Pietà*, Michelangelo gave the Virgin an expression of peaceful acceptance, rather than one distorted by the horror of the Crucifixion. With her face softly outlined by the gentle folds of her head covering, Mary seems to accept the inevitable, and in so doing, moves beyond the tragedy of death.

Visitors who see Michelangelo's *Pietà* in Saint

Michelangelo's Pietà

Peter's Basilica frequently note the inscription on a narrow band that crosses from the Virgin's left shoulder to her waist. The words, "Michelangelo Buonarroti, Florentine, made this," attest to the youthful sculptor's confidence in his ability as well as his fierce defensiveness. Having overheard someone attribute his work to another artist, Michelangelo had stolen into the *basilica* during the night and carved his signature!

The *Pietà* firmly established Michelangelo's genius. Vasari said, "It is a miracle that a stone without shape should have been reduced to such perfection." Michelangelo was 23 when he began work on the *Pietà*. In the years to come, he would create countless works of art, but none would surpass his *Pietà* in beauty, grace, and promise of eternal life.

In the spring of 1501, Michelangelo returned to Florence. For the time being, the city was in a state of relative calm and a republican government had been reestablished. He was not long in finding a new contract, an agreement to begin work on fifteen small statues for a cardinal's tomb in Siena. But the three-year contract was soon broken—one of many in the artist's career and the only one of his own choosing. The reason lay in the fact that a greater challenge had presented itself.

Before his return from Rome, Michelangelo

had received letters from friends suggesting that, in Vasari's words, "if he came back, he might have the big piece of marble that Piero Soderini, the *gonfaloniere* (official head of the city), had talked of giving to Leonardo da Vinci, but was now proposing to present to Andrea Sansovino, an excellent sculptor, who was making every effort to get it."

The stone, a huge chunk of pure white unflawed Carrara marble 18 feet in height, had been discarded by an earlier artist and had been in the cathedral's work yard for 35 years. Ideas previously submitted to the cathedral's Board of Works had all been rejected and the Giant, as it was called, lay idle.

Michelangelo submitted a proposal to the cathedral Board that he had been considering for some time. Then, knowing that the Board weighed its decisions slowly, he signed the contract for the Siena statues. By the middle of August, however, just as he had completed his initial plans for the cardinal's tomb, Michelangelo received word that Soderini and the Board had granted him the Giant.

At dawn on September 13, 1501, Michelangelo began work on his next great achievement, the colossal figure of the young David of biblical lore. With his customary insistence upon secrecy, he had ordered his workmen to build a wooden shed around the marble block, which would be his "earthly prison" until the *David* was completed. During that time, he worked at a fevered pace, sleeping in his clothes in a rented room near the churchyard and isolating himself from the rest of the world as he set free from "the living stone" the image that he believed lay within.

Condivi gives us a visual impression of the young man working within the confines of the *David* enclosure:

> Michelangelo is of good complexion, more muscular ... than fat or fleshy in his person: healthy above all things, as well by reason of his natural constitution as of the exercise he takes ... his countenance always shows a good and wholesome color. Of stature he is as follows: height [medium] broad in the shoulders, the rest of the body somewhat slender ... the shape of his face is oval ... the nose a little flattened ... the hair of the head is black, as also the beard.

At the age of 26, Michelangelo had begun to acquire those characteristics by which he would later be identified—those eccentricities of temperament and habit that frequently impressed people as strange and inhospitable. At times, the artist appeared excessively optimistic and on other occasions disturbingly melancholy. The *David* exemplified his brighter nature and his eagerness to take on a seemingly impossible challenge.

Throughout his life, Michelangelo possessed deep feelings of insecurity, and yet, he was totally confident in his genius and eager—at times boastful—to display his artistic powers. He relished fame yet hid himself from it. He sought recognition yet complained of his lack of privacy. Late in life, he would comment, "The vanished years, alas, I do not find among them all one day that I could call my own."

Although the artist enthusiastically believed that he could do whatever he set his heart on doing, he constantly fell behind in his schedule and in his commitments. One writer has suggested that because of this, Michelangelo was aware that he was failing his patrons as well as himself, and that these failings contributed to his melancholy. These and other factors—including his lifelong battle to prove himself worthy to his dependent father and brothers—contributed to the complex character of this remarkable Renaissance man.

From the moment Michelangelo began working on the *David*, he removed himself from the trivialities of the practical world and was critical of any interference that might break his concentration. Resentful of the constant barrage of letters from his father and brothers begging for money—yet eager to grant their every wish—he once wrote, "I have written you several times that every time I have a letter of yours I get a headache." On another occasion he

pleaded, "I no longer know what you want from me . . . don't write me anymore, because you keep me from working."

Of Michelangelo's habits while working, Condivi wrote: "He has always been extremely temperate in living, using food more because it was necessary than for any pleasure he took in it, especially when he was engaged upon some great work, for then he usually confined himself to a piece of bread, which he ate in the middle of his labor."

When involved in a major project such as the *David*, the artist's creative energies were so intense that he slept fitfully and sparingly. He found sleep disturbing, no doubt because he found that it interrupted his work, but also because he suffered from severe head and stomach pains while asleep.

During those infrequent periods when Michelangelo was not under the pressure of a contract deadline, he would occasionally invite a friend for an evening meal and a round of intellectual discussion. These conversations were spirited, with much talk about the politics of the day. There was also much analyzing of Dante and Petrarch, the two great poets and essayists who profoundly influenced him throughout his life.

The food was simple. When far from Florence, Michelangelo had his nephew, Lionardo (a merchant), send him the sweet wines of Tuscany—usually the mellow white trebbiano of which the artist was particularly fond—and marzolino cheese, which he described as "most delicious."

Always generous, Michelangelo shared his food bounty with an assortment of people—from cardinals and popes to visiting relatives and laborers. From countless notes—generally accompanied by lovely little illustrations likely intended for a cook who was illiterate—we know that Michelangelo kept to a distinct pattern when planning his menus. For an honored guest, he would suggest a salad, four breads, two wines, a plate of spinach, four anchovies, and a pasta. For a stonecutter or helper, he requested six breads, two bowls of fennel soup, one herring, and wine. And when he dined alone, he required only two breads, wine, a herring, and pasta.

From his biographers and a few intimates, a clear picture emerges of the extraordinary methods Michelangelo used as he worked on the

David—the same methods that he applied to all of his great achievements. One eyewitness described the sculptor as he knocked "more chips out of the hardest marble in a quarter of an hour than three . . . masons could have done in an hour. . . . With one blow he would remove chips as thick as three or four fingers, and his aim was so accurate that had he but chipped off a little more all might have been ruined."

This frenzied pace seemed to typify the driving forces behind each of Michelangelo's creations. These forces supplied him with the creative energy to draw from the stone that idea—that image—that his mind's eye could see. The artist took much pleasure in making his work seem effortless, yet from the countless sketches in existence it is obvious that he made many drawings in preparation for each project, working and reworking a figure until he was satisfied. Along with these sketches, Michelangelo often worked with clay or wax to produce small figures, which he called *bozzétti*, or "buds," concentrating on the minute aspects of the human form—fingernails, wrinkles, and veins. Toward the end of his life, he destroyed all the small figures that were not up to his rigid standards of perfection.

Michelangelo frequently used live models from which he could sketch every detail of human anatomy accurately. With his extensive knowledge of the human form, he analyzed line, proportion, and balance, commenting that "it is necessary to keep one's compass in one's eyes and not in the hand, for the hands execute, but the eye judges."

"The hands execute, but the eye judges."

For three years, the artist labored over the huge block of marble, his hammer and chisels giving shape and intensity to the misshapen Giant that would become the *David*. At the time, he was unaware that his marble sculpture, along with the great paintings of other Italian artists, would usher in a new era called the High Renaissance, in which all the artistic achievements of the fifteenth century became stepping stones toward the great works that were to come. No longer would art imitate nature in a stilted and highly stylized manner. Instead, art would *record* nature as the artist observed it.

Michelangelo, however, infused his realism with abstract concepts. The *David* also stood for an idea—the triumph of good over evil. It represented youthful energy and courage overcoming brute force. That idea is evident in the taut lines of David's body, the twist of the muscles, the head turned to face overwhelming odds, and the tense

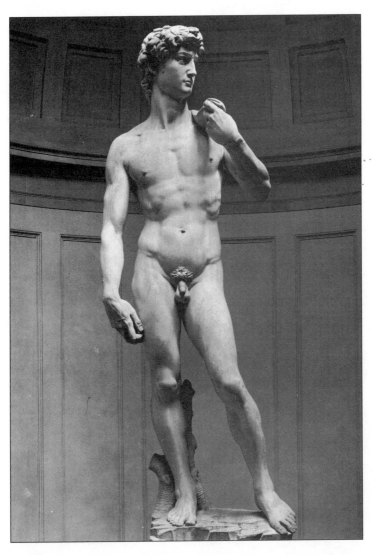

With the David, *Michelangelo demonstrated his mastery of the human form.*

neck muscles revealing an emotionally charged moment.

When the *David* was finished, the wooden enclosure was torn away to reveal the sculpture in all of its immensity and perfection. Soon it would be enveloped in a sling inside a framework of

David's face reveals the tension and emotion in the moment before he kills Goliath.

planks supported by a windlass (a device used in those times to raise or haul objects) and rollers. Then it would be painstakingly hauled, with the aid of forty men, to the courtyard entrance of the City Hall where crowds of awed Florentines gathered "to gaze and to admire." Vasari observed, "This work has carried off the palm [a symbol of highest praise] from all other statues, past and present."

CHAPTER 5

WIELDING THE PEN

For some time now, Michelangelo had been experimenting with poetry. Since his years with the Medicis, he had studied the works of his favorite Italian poets, Dante and Petrarch. His first poems, written in the sonnet form that was popular in his day, reflect Petrarch's influence.

The artist's poetic works were concerned with his emotions. He wrote of his love for things earthly and divine, the painful frustration of falling short of his goals, his fears of death, and his hopes that a merciful God would release him from the sins of a lifetime. In his poems, Michelangelo frequently made reference to a divinity that he believed guided all his work:

> If my rough hammer shapes human aspects
> out of the hard rock, now this one, now that,
> It is held and guided by Divine Fiat [order]
> lending it motion, moving as He elects.

Yet despite his faith in this divine being, Michelangelo struggled—not only in the same poem, but throughout his life—with the failure of his earthly "hammer" to achieve the perfection that matched his original idea:

> I unfinished am and all undone . . . unless
> the Divine Smith [Creator] should deign to
> anoint me and help me, alone here below.

In other verses, Michelangelo's voice was filled with love and yearning for a fair young maid:

> A wreath with flowers, happy and well braided
> on someone's golden brow, is so rejoiced,
> One's by the other past another thrust,
> As if to be the first to kiss her head.

Unlike the poems that unveiled Michelangelo's inner struggles, fears, and conflicts, his immense volume of letters (more than five hundred of them) reveals a far more public persona. Written over the span of sixty-seven years or more, they reveal the thoughts of an artist beset by the whims and fancies of a conniving family who relied on the financial rewards of his talents, while at the same time barely acknowledging them. The letters are practical in nature and deal with everyday concerns—the unreliable habits of workers, financial matters, acquisition of properties, family problems, and here and there, some amusing suggestions to a nephew in search of a bride.

In the letters, Michelangelo advises, urges, complains, finds himself cheated, and criticizes family members for their shortcomings. He is frequently grumpy and suspicious of unfair treatment (particularly in his dealings with Pope Julius II), yet in many instances, he is remarkably generous and thoughtful. Throughout the writings, there is evidence of the constant stress under which Michelangelo worked—partly because of the demands he placed upon himself— but also because of goals unrealized and promises broken.

One of the earliest letters, dated December 19, 1506, when the artist was working in Bologna, is addressed to Buonarroto, Michelangelo's favorite brother. An excerpt reads:

> . . . I understand all about your affairs and Giovansimone's [the artist's ne'er-do-well brother]. I am glad he is going into your shop and that he wants to do well, because I want to help him like the rest of you. . . . as for the money that you write me Giovansimone wants to invest in a shop, I feel he should delay four months more.

Three years later, in a letter addressed to his father (who was obviously annoyed at not having

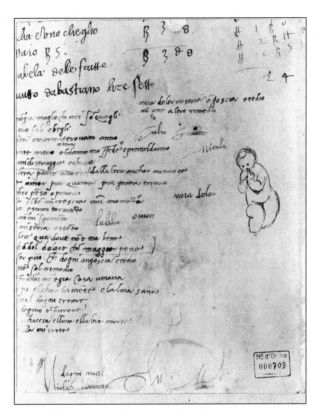

As he had with painting and sculpture, Michelangelo used writing to express his emotions. This page contains one of his sonnets.

heard from his son for some time) while working on the Sistine Chapel ceiling, he wrote:

I learn from your last how it has been said there that I am dead. It's a thing that matters little, since I am really alive ... I am attending to work as much as I can. It's now thirteen months since I've had money from the Pope [Julius II]. ... I am unhappy and not in too good health staying here, and with a great deal of work, no instructions, and no money. But I have good hopes God will help me. Give my greetings to ... [friends in Florence].

"It has been said there that I am dead."

On one occasion, an infuriated Michelangelo wrote to his father:

Most revered father: I learned from your last how things are going with Giovansimone. For ten years I have not heard worse news, because I believed I had their affairs all set, that is, in such a way they could hope to have a good shop with my help as I promised them, and in that hope attend to making something of themselves ... if he removes anything from the house worth a pin, or does anything else you don't like, please let me know. ... I want you to know that all the labors I have always endured were for you no less than for myself, and what I have bought I bought so that it would be yours for as long as you lived.

In October 1542, Michelangelo delayed work on frescoes in a Vatican chapel named for Pope Paul III because of confusion over a contract, apparently about money owed him. An angry and extremely frustrated Michelangelo addressed one of the Vatican cardinals:

Your lordship sends to tell me that I should paint and have no doubts. I answer that painting is done with the brain, not the hands and one who cannot have his brains about him dishonors himself, so until my affairs are straight I can do nothing.

"Painting is done with the brain, not the hands."

In 1547, however, a fatherly Michelangelo advised his nephew on matters concerning a wife:

I wrote you about getting married and informed you about three girls who had been spoken of to me here . . . I remind you that between husband and wife there should always be at least ten years' difference, and to take care that besides being good she is healthy.

Again, on the subject of marriage, the artist generously offered money for a new house:

> I would be very glad if before you got married you bought a nicer and roomier house than the one where you are now living, and I would send you the money.

In one of Michelangelo's last letters, addressed to his friend Giorgio Vasari, he described his grief over the death of his faithful servant, Urbino:

> I can write only with difficulty. . . . you know that Urbino is dead, which for me was a very great mercy of God, but my heavy hurt and infinite sorrow. The mercy is that he kept me alive. . . . I had him twenty-six years and found him most loyal and faithful. . . . I am filled with such grief at thoughts like this that I cannot write.

"I am filled with such grief at thoughts like this that I cannot write."

CHAPTER 6

A CALL FROM ROME

After completing the *David*, Michelangelo accepted commissions for other works. One of these was
a life-size *Madonna and Child*, a marble sculpture of remarkable grace. Michelangelo remembered the scoldings of a radical priest, Savonarola,
who had once criticized the costumed Madonnas
of an earlier period as being unrealistic. He took
care to clothe his newest Madonna in the hooded
mantle of a young peasant woman, much as he
had done with the *Pietà*. The result was a pair of
figures that moved far beyond the conventions of
fifteenth-century artists.

The beauty of the *Bruges Madonna*, as the
work is often called, lies in the solemnity of the
mother and child, as though each is aware of the
tragedy that will one day take place. The Madonna's head is turned away from her son, her eyes
downcast in grave submission to the inevitable.

In the Bruges Madonna, *Michelangelo took care to clothe Mary in the garb of a peasant.*

Her left arm is protective, her right hand holds a book—destiny foretold? The child's expression—equally somber—suggests total acceptance of the fate that will be his.

As a wedding gift for his friends Angelo Doni and Maddalena Strozzi, Michelangelo completed the lovely *Doni Madonna*, a painting on wood, circular in shape, depicting the Holy Family. During this same period, Michelangelo worked on yet another *Madonna and Child*, an indication of his continuing interest in the subject of the Virgin Mary and Christ.

In April 1503, the Cathedral Board of Florence offered Michelangelo a contract for twelve larger-than-life statues of the apostles. The artist accepted the commission and set to work on his sketches and models. But soon after he began carving the figure of Matthew, Piero Soderini, the city's chief executive, ordered Michelangelo to set aside the contract and instead paint a *mural* of a historic Florentine event, the Battle of Cascina, on the wall of the council chamber in the Palazzo Vecchio. The contract, as designed by Soderini, was to be in the form of a competition between Michelangelo and Leonardo da Vinci, the prolific artist and inventor who was more than twenty years Michelangelo's senior.

Leonardo had recently returned from a stay in Milan where he had completed the *Last Supper*.

Promptly settling into his work, he began mixing the colors for his fresco, using techniques similar to those he had used in the Milan painting. But sadly, Leonardo's work was a dismal failure. He had tried a mixture of oil, varnish, and pigment that would not dry, and the paint on large areas of the wall ran. Giving up in disgust, Leonardo abandoned the project and turned to another of his many pursuits. Not long after, Michelangelo was called to Rome by Pope Julius II.

When Julius II became pope in 1503, he had three major goals: to rebuild the church's secular and political power, to replenish the Vatican's treasury, and to recover the splendor that had once been Rome. Hoping to unify all of Italy's fractious city-states, his ultimate aim was to bring most of Europe under the control of the Vatican. And Rome, at the center of this new empire, would become the richest and most beautiful city in the world.

For two years, Julius II had been gathering Italy's leading artists and architects in Rome. But when Michelangelo arrived there during the spring of 1505, he discovered to his dismay that the pope had no specific plans for him. Julius, having deprived the young artist of his contracts with the city of Florence, simply wanted him on hand until he thought of a project for him.

But Julius hadn't reckoned with the likes of

Michelangelo Buonarroti. As the historian John Addington Symonds once commented, "Both [men] aimed at colossal achievements in their respective fields. Both were *uomini terribili*, to use an Italian phrase denoting vigor of character and energy of genius, made formidable by an abrupt, uncompromising spirit." Both had met their match in what someone once suggested were the combined qualities of "intensity and determination."

> **"Both [men] aimed at colossal achievements in their respective fields."**

The relationship between Michelangelo and his newly acquired patron would indeed become formidable. For ten stormy years, the two sparred with each other, winning—and then losing—battles that would continue to rage until Julius's death soon after the completion of the Sistine Chapel ceiling. The relationship lasted because, despite their differences, the two men needed one another. Julius II, for all of his wielding of Vatican power, depended upon Michelangelo's versatile genius to achieve his goals. And as a famous historian observed, without Julius II "Michelangelo might never have had the opportunity of developing the full power of his imagination."

Condivi continues the story: "At last it

*Dynamic, arrogant, powerful, Julius II was
determined to reclaim Rome's former glory for
both himself and the Church.*

occurred to [Julius] to use [Michelangelo's] genius in the construction of his own tomb. The design furnished by Michelangelo pleased the pope so much that he sent him off immediately to Carrara, with a commission to quarry as much marble as was needful."

The ancient marble quarries of Carrara lie in northwestern Italy in the Apuan Alps. Here, where today the blast of explosives are capable of releasing tons of crystallized limestone for shipment of the beautiful black, white, gray, or streaked stone to points throughout the world, Michelangelo spent almost a year selecting the finest examples he could find. He was happy there, in the environment of his early years.

Michelangelo himself selected each piece of marble. He knew what to look for and what to reject. As in everything, he was a perfectionist who knew not only his art but his trade. Returning to Rome, Michelangelo made arrangements for the placement of the marble blocks. As Condivi wrote, "He had . . . the stone blocks disembarked and carried to the Piazza of St. Peter's behind San Caterina, where he kept his lodging, close to the corridor connecting the [Vatican] Palace with the Castel

_____

"Julius indeed began to heap favors upon Michelangelo."

_____

Sant'Angelo. The quantity of stone was enormous so that, when it was all spread out upon the square it stirred amazement in the minds of most folk, but joy in the Pope's. Julius indeed began to heap favors upon Michelangelo for when he had begun to work, the Pope used frequently to betake of himself to his house, conversing there with him about the tomb and about other works which he proposed to carry out. . . . In order to arrive more conveniently at Michelangelo's lodgings, he had a drawbridge thrown across the corridor, by which he might gain [private] access."

For the tomb of Julius II, Michelangelo had drawn plans for a colossal structure that would satisfy the enormous ego and pride of his patron yet also throw light upon his own skills and creative inventiveness. Michelangelo envisioned the tomb as his greatest sculptural masterpiece and a challenge to all who followed him. During the next thirty-seven years, however, what Condivi referred to as "the tragedy of the tomb" would continue to frustrate and plague its designer, causing him to become captive to threats and delays, broken contracts and recriminations by the pope and an assortment of his enemies and heirs. "In bondage to this tomb," an aging Michelangelo would later admit, "I lost

"In bondage to this tomb, I lost all of my youth."

all of my youth." In fact, he considered the business of the tomb to be the greatest tragedy of his long and illustrious career.

As a tribute to all of Julius's accomplishments, Michelangelo designed a tomb of astonishing proportions. Measuring 36 feet long and 24 feet wide, it was to be shaped like a step-pyramid, rising to a height of 36 feet. It would be self-standing and embellished with no less than forty larger-than-life statues. In his description of the plan, Condivi wrote, "At the summit, two angels supported a sarcophagus [stone coffin]. One . . . appeared to smile, rejoicing that the soul of the Pope had been received among the blessed spirits, the other seemed to weep, as [if] sorrowing that the world had been robbed of such a man."

The coffin was actually symbolic, because a chamber at the base of the tomb enclosed a chapel "in the midst of which was a marble chest wherein the corpse of the Pope was . . . to be deposited." No single work of burial art since the days of the Roman Emperor Caesar Augustus could compare with its elegance or splendor. With customary exuberance and drive, Michelangelo predicted that he would complete the work—tomb, sarcophagus and forty statues—in five years.

The sculptor saw only one problem. If the tomb were to be self-standing, it would need space. St. Peter's Basilica was not big enough to house such a monument, and it would not do to have a tomb of such grandeur placed outdoors. After considerable thought, the pope himself solved the dilemma: the old basilica was falling apart—so build a new one!

Satisfied for the moment that the tomb project was well in hand and excited by the idea of a glorious new basilica to show it off, Julius turned to thoughts of politics and preparations for a military campaign. Months passed and Michelangelo, sensing a change in the pope's mood and concerned that he had not been paid for some time, called on his patron. Arriving at the papal apartments, Michelangelo announced his presence. But to his shock and humiliation, the artist was told that His Holiness refused to see him.

"He had me turned away by a groom," Michelangelo reported to a friend. "A bishop, seeing this, said: 'Do you not know who that man is?' The groom replied to me: 'Excuse me, sir, I have orders to do this.'"

A furious Michelangelo flew out of the building and hastily scribbled a note to the pontiff: "Most Blessed Father, I have been turned out of your Palace today by your orders wherefore I give you notice that from this time forward, if you want me, you must look for me elsewhere than at Rome." With this, he ordered his servants to sell all of his furniture, "and on the second hour of the night, set out on post horses" for Florence. "I was sent packing," Michelangelo wrote to a friend, "and the fellow who turned me away knew who I was."

Hearing of Michelangelo's departure, Julius quickly sent emissaries to follow him and bring him back to Rome. But the artist rode with such speed that he arrived in Florence before the men could overtake him.

Julius issued three papal briefs to Piero Soderini in Florence, but despite these demands Michelangelo refused to budge. In the months that followed, he worked on the fresco at the Palazzo Vecchio and considered leaving the country to take up a commission with the Turks, who were tempting him with offers. Soderini, fearing the pope's wrath, pleaded with the sculptor to return to Rome.

For a time, Michelangelo remained resolute. But in May 1506, he wrote to his friend Giuliano da Sangallo in Rome: "I have learned from your [letter] how the Pope took my departure badly. . . . Read this to the Pope and His Holiness should know that I am more disposed than ever to go on with this work."

Michelangelo's letter to Sangallo dealt with issues other than money. Pride was one, stubbornness another. The primary issue, however, had to do with the combative natures of two giants engaged in fierce confrontation. Neither wished to give in to the other. On the night the sculptor had fled from Rome one of the pope's emissaries had carried an ultimatum: "Come back at once to Rome, under penalty of our displeasure." The warning from His Holiness had gone unheeded.

"Come back at once to Rome, under penalty of our displeasure."

In the end, it was Piero Soderini who settled the dispute. Summoning Michelangelo to his quarters, a city official warned him: "You have tried a bout with the Pope on which the King of France would not have ventured. . . . We do not wish to go to war on your account. . . . Make up your mind to return."

Reflecting on the matter, Michelangelo relented. He would see the pope and offer his apologies. He would travel to Bologna, however, rather than Rome. His Holiness was once again on the move.

In August of that year, Julius II had launched a military campaign against Bologna and Perugia, two of the troublesome city-states that challenged the authority of Rome. Determined to impress his vassals with the stateliness of his office, the pope arrived in Perugia with a spectacular array of 12 cardinals and their entourage, 500 knights in gleaming armor astride magnificent stallions, and 300 highly trained guardsmen.

Julius's army halted first at Perugia, prepared for battle against the formidable tyrant Giampaolo Baglioni, whose bloody exploits were feared throughout Italy. Faced with the pope's glorious retinue, Baglioni gave in without so much as a skirmish and even offered to contribute troops to the papal army. When word of the uneventful surrender reached Bologna, its leaders fled and the city offered no resistance. Julius made his triumphant entry on November 11. Ten days later, the pope summoned Michelangelo to the government palace in Bologna.

A humbled Michelangelo arrived at the city soon after, stopping first at the cathedral to attend mass. There he was recognized by papal authorities and taken to the pope's quarters. Condivi described the highly charged scene: "When the Pope beheld him, his face clouded with anger, and he cried, 'It was your duty to come to seek us, and you have waited till we came to seek you.'" Michelangelo fell at Julius's feet, exposing a noose that he had bound about his neck as a token of submission, praying loudly for a pardon and

"It was your duty to come to seek us, and you have waited till we came to seek you."

"pleading in his excuse that he had not erred through forwardness but through great distress of mind. . . . The Pope remained holding his head low and answering nothing, evidently much agitated, when a certain prelate sent by Cardinal Soderini [brother of Piero Soderini] to put in a good word for Michelangelo, came forward and said: 'Your Holiness might overlook his fault; he did wrong through ignorance. These painters, outside their art, are all like this.'"

The pope stared at the cardinal in indignation. Condivi continued: "The Pope answered in a fury: 'It is you, not I, who are insulting him. It is you, not he, who are the ignoramus and the rascal. Get hence out of my sight and bad luck to you.' When the fellow did not move, he was cast forth by the servants, as Michelangelo used to relate, with good round kicks and thumpings. So the Pope, having spent the surplus of his bile [anger] upon the [Cardinal], took Michelangelo aside and pardoned him.

"Not long afterwards he sent for him and said: 'I wish you to make my statue on a large scale in bronze. I intend to place it on the facade of San Petronio [Bologna's cathedral].'"

Julius gave a description of what he had in mind: the bronze was to be of immense proportion—a seated figure measuring ten feet in height. Wishing no further argument, Michelangelo quietly agreed to his patron's command.

Before leaving for Rome, Julius placed a generous deposit of 1,000 ducats in the sculptor's account. Condivi wrote, "But before [the Pope] did so, Michelangelo had made the clay model. Being somewhat in doubt how to manage the left hand, after making the Pope give the benediction with the right, he asked Julius, who had come to see the statue, if he would like it to hold a book. 'What book?' replied he. 'A sword! I know nothing about letters, not I.' Jesting then about the right hand, which was vehement in action, he said with a smile to Michelangelo: 'That statue of yours, is it blessing or cursing?' To which the sculptor replied: 'Holy Father, it is threatening the people of Bologna if they are not prudent.'" For the moment, Michelangelo and His Holiness were at peace.

While Julius and his entourage were returning to Rome in stately splendor, Michelangelo concentrated on completing the model for the bronze figure. Toying a bit with the pontiff's request for a sword, he worked out the problem by instead placing the keys of Saint Peter in the left hand of the statue. Working with bronze was troublesome because it was not a medium the sculptor was comfortable with. And, due to miscalculation, the money on deposit from the pope was insufficient.

As work on the bronze continued, conditions worsened. The weather in Bologna was unbearably hot, and a plague swept through the city. Quarrels broke out with Michelangelo's laborers. One walked off the job, and another was fired for incompetence. Filled with frustration and longing to return to Rome and the project of Julius's tomb, a tormented Michelangelo wrote home once again: "If I were to make another [bronze] statue I do not think I would be able to survive it."

"If I were to make another [bronze] statue I do not think I would be able to survive it."

Despite his troubles with the Bologna assignment, *Julius the Colossus*, with its full regalia of pontifical vestments and triple tiara, was hauled to its place above the main entrance of the cathedral on February 21, 1508. Its glory, however was short-lived. Three years later, Bologna's defeated leaders, who had fled from Julius's advances, would march back into the city, tear down the statue of Julius II, and send it crashing to the ground. The bronze would be sold as scrap and melted into cannon. The image of a proud Julius would be toppled, and Michelangelo's labor of more than a year would come to nothing.

Exhausted from his work on the pope's statue, Michelangelo left Bologna and returned to Florence, concerned about his family because political upheavals had the city in turmoil once again. Arriving in Florence during March 1508, the sculptor hoped to resume work on the Cascina fresco in the Palazzo Vecchio and perhaps to recover his contract for the Twelve Apostles. But that was not to be.

Julius II, having launched a series of political and military movements that would keep much of Italy in a state of unrest for the next 4½ years, was back in Rome with a new plan for the artistic glorification of the Vatican.

To fulfill this wish, he summoned Michelangelo.

CHAPTER 7

THE SISTINE CHAPEL

"I record how on this day, the 10th of May, 1508, I, Michelangelo, sculptor, have received from the Holiness of our Lord Pope Julius II, 500 ducats . . . on account of the painting of the vault [ceiling] of the Sistine Chapel, on which I begin to work."

And so it was that Michelangelo Buonarroti noted in his journal an agreement that would cause him anguish, frustration, humiliation, and fury. An indication of the troubles that would plague the artist for the next 4½ years lay in the manner by which he signed the record of his new contract: "I, Michelangelo, *sculptor*."

"I, Michelangelo, sculptor."

This diverse genius, who would one day be

acclaimed in so many fields of endeavor, saw himself as a sculptor—no more, no less. For this reason, and because he had little experience (other than his work on the *Battle of Cascina* in Florence) in the art of fresco painting, Michelangelo was reluctant to accept the contract from Julius.

There was another reason for the artist's concern. In ordering Michelangelo to Rome, the pope had stated that he wanted to discuss certain matters. Michelangelo assumed that Julius wanted him to resume work on the tomb project, which had been postponed because of the contract for the bronze colossus. Now it seemed there would be yet another delay.

In the weeks that followed, Michelangelo concentrated on his preliminary sketches for the ceiling. Julius had granted him complete freedom to draft his own design, and he spent long hours considering the enormity of the area he was to paint as well as the history of the chapel and the purpose for which it was built.

Designed by a Florentine architect in 1475, the Sistine Chapel has an interior that matches the exact dimensions of the Jerusalem Temple described in the Bible. The floor of the nave is of multicolored Italian marble set in a rich *mosaic* pattern, and the ceiling consists of a flattened *barrel vault* (a masonry ceiling that is arched). On either side, a series of six gracefully arched windows representing the Twelve Apostles rise above paneled frescoes painted by a number of great Tuscan and Umbrian artists, including Botticelli, Perugino, Signorelli, and Michelangelo's first teacher, Domenico Ghirlandaio. The frescoes depict two important cycles from the Old and New Testaments—the *Life of Moses* and the *Life of Christ*. Niches set between the twelve windows and elsewhere along the walls contain elegant early Renaissance portraits of a series of Roman pontiffs. (A fresco of Christ and the first three popes was later destroyed to make room for Michelangelo's final masterpiece for the Chapel, the *Last Judgment*). In harmony with Pope Sixtus's wishes, the entire architectural and artistic design of the chapel brought together all of the significant periods in the church's history from the earliest days of Christianity.

Michelangelo's initial plan for the ceiling centered on twelve larger-than-life figures representing the apostles. This idea had been suggested by Julius. But Michelangelo soon balked, preferring a design that included biblical scenes. Julius agreed and drew up a new contract granting Michelangelo complete control of the project.

When Michelangelo had completed his sketches for the ceiling, he built a platform that towered eighty feet above the floor of the chapel. Then sometime in late December 1508 or January of the following year, he climbed the framework to begin the first of the nine episodes from the Book of Genesis.

From the start, the venture seemed doomed to failure. Condivi wrote that the artist had hardly begun painting before he encountered serious problems:

"The work began to throw out mold to such an extent that the figures could hardly be seen through it. Michelangelo thought that this excuse might be sufficient to get him relieved of the whole job. So he went to the Pope and said: 'I already told Your Holiness that painting is not my trade. What I have done is spoiled—if you do not believe it, send to see.' The Pope sent Sangallo who, after inspecting the fresco, pronounced that the lime base had been put on too wet, and that water oozing out produced this moldy surface. He told Michelangelo what the cause was, and bade him proceed with the work. So the excuse helped him nothing."

"I already told Your Holiness that painting is not my trade."

By now, totally convinced that there was no escape from the task, Michelangelo threw himself into learning the techniques of fresco painting.

Calling upon five acquaintances from his early days in Florence (including his old friend Francesco Granacci), he asked them to teach him all that he needed to know.

In a short time, however, the artist's standards for perfection caused him to be severely critical of the others' work. His own initial attempts infuriated him even further. Before long, an enraged Michelangelo dismissed the entire group, including Granacci. During the days that followed, he destroyed everyone else's painting, barred the chapel to all but the pope and a scant few admitted by special permission, and resolved that all further work on the ceiling would be carried out by himself.

For the next four years, the artist pressed on, refusing even the help of the usual *garzóni* (laborers). Although he was often in pain, he was determined to complete the work: "I strain more than any man who ever lived . . . and with great exhaustion and yet I have the patience to arrive at the desired goal."

"I strain more than any man who ever lived."

Michelangelo's extraordinary efforts found their reward in the final achievement, which presents a powerfully coherent drama as one scene of Genesis flows swiftly into the next. Throughout the vast expanse of the Sistine ceiling there is a sense of action as the figures within each frame move forward through the course of time.

The nine episodes of the Creation story are clearly divided into three major groups, beginning with the origins of the Universe, Man, and Evil. The first group includes the *Separation of Light from Darkness,* the *Creation of Sun, Moon, and Planets,* the *Separation of the Waters from the Land,* and the *Creation of the Animals.* In the second group, the supreme force of the Creator's energy flows from a single outstretched finger— poised as if to send an electrical charge of life through the body of a reclining Adam, whose arm and finger are similarly outstretched to receive that power. Scenes of the *Fall and the Expulsion* vibrate with the conflicting images of Good pitted against Evil. In the final group, the drama of the Great Flood engulfs a mass of humanity struggling to reach Noah's craft.

A vibrant but curious feature in Michelangelo's story of the Creation is the presence of the ignudi, a series of colossal nudes that seem to represent the purity of humanity created in the image and likeness of God. They act as observers to the unfolding scenes, swept up in a variety of emotions ranging from contemplation to despair, and from resignation to terror—aware of the drama of Life, yet powerless to intervene.

Adam awaits the touch of life from God.

In the center of the Sistine Chapel ceiling, Michelangelo painted one of his most famous images: God creating Adam. Surrounded by a host of angels, God approaches Adam, extending the finger that will give Adam life. Adam sits limply on the earth, his naked body displaying the glory of the human form. He gazes weakly but longingly at the Lord, waiting for the divine spark that will animate his soul. No other image in Western art captures humanity's potential for the divine so beautifully and powerfully.

Around the middle of the Sistine ceiling sit the prophets and the sibyls (female prophets of classical mythology), each on a huge throne with ornamental scrolls that identify them. With these figures, Michelangelo joins in harmony the contrasting elements of the Judeo-Christian world of the Old Testament and the pagan world of Greek and Roman mythology. In the prophets and the sibyls, the artist saw the "unceasing hope of the redemption of mankind."

In his *Ancestors of Christ*, a relatively unknown section of the Sistine ceiling, Michelangelo worked on eight Old Testament scenes which dealt with some of his favorite themes: the saving of the Hebrews through divine intervention and prophesies that told of the coming of a Messiah. In these frescoes, the artist's purpose was to provide a clear connection to the earlier paintings on the wall below them, which illustrate the *Life of Moses* and *Life of Christ*.

During the time that Michelangelo labored on the Sistine ceiling, his face and beard were speckled with paint and his cramped body stiff with pain. He lived a solitary existence, so deeply involved with his work that he barely took time to eat. Letters from his family in Florence com-

The Delphic Sibyl

plained of his neglect of them, and brothers and friends journeying to Rome frequently found themselves turned away. His life was his art—and his art came before everything.

Michelangelo's spiritual and artistic growth

during this time was extraordinary. In the earliest frescoes the artist's misgivings about his work are clear. His portrayal of Noah's ark is crowded with figures. He had not yet mastered "the feeling for open space." Yet, as in everything else that Michelangelo attempted, he grasped new techniques with amazing speed.

As he crossed the ceiling, Michelangelo became increasingly sure of himself. The scenes of God creating the universe are dominated by massive figure painted in bold, vigorous strokes. The size of the ignudi, prophets, and sibyls increased so dramatically that he had to lower the pedestals on which they sat to give them more space. The ignudi, twisting and turning out of their original corners, soon overlapped the scenes they were supposedly observing. As his confidence grew, the artist worked faster and faster. It is believed that during the final phase of the work—a period of about three months—Michelangelo completed a section of the ceiling as large as an area he had taken three years to paint!

Despite his remarkable evolution as a fresco artist, Michelangelo continued to be plagued by self-doubt. To make matters worse, Michelangelo was also in a constant state of anxiety about his relationship with the pope. During Julius's visits to examine the progress of the ceiling, the artist often found him impatient and demanding. On more than one occasion, the tension between the two exploded into a stubborn battle of wills. At one point, when the ceiling was only half finished, the pope ordered that the doors to the chapel be opened to the public, and Michelangelo was forced to cope with mobs of excited Romans milling about on the floor below him.

Sometime toward the end of his arduous labor on the ceiling, Michelangelo asked the pontiff for time off and a little money to visit his family in Florence. The republic had been overthrown and a new generation of Medicis had seized control, ousting many of their former allies. Michelangelo was greatly concerned about the well-being of his father and brothers. Julius was enraged: "Well, what about this chapel? When will it be finished?"

"Well, what about this chapel? When will it be finished?"

Michelangelo answered impatiently, "When I can, Holy Father."

The pope turned and swung wildly with his cane, striking the artist with a hard blow. "When I can! When I can! . . . I will soon make you finish it!"

With this, an infuriated Michelangelo fled the chapel and raced home.

It took 500 crowns and a written apology to persuade Michelangelo to return to the chapel and complete his work.

Michelangelo's paintings cover the
Sistine Chapel ceiling.

"I will soon make you finish it!"

On October 31, 1512, four-and-a-half years after he had begun to map out his original design, the doors to the Sistine Chapel were thrown open. Vasari wrote, "The whole world came running to see what Michelangelo had done . . . and certainly it was such as to make everyone speechless with astonishment."

CHAPTER 8

MOURNING FOR THE POPE

In February 1513, less than four months after Michelangelo had completed work on the Sistine Chapel ceiling, Julius II died. Although no records of the artist's reaction to the pope's death have been found, there is no doubt that he felt a deep sense of loss. The two men, despite their habitual sparring, had a loyalty to one another. Vasari commented, "Michelangelo knew the Pope and was, after all, much attached to him."

One thing was certain: Michelangelo saw the pope's death as further reason to complete the unfinished tomb in honor of the man who, despite his complex nature, had accomplished much for the Papal States. Shortly after Julius's death, Michelangelo had an important meeting with Cardinal Aginensis, Julius's nephew and the executor of his estate. A new contract was promised, enabling the artist to construct an even more elaborate tomb, allowing him seven years to complete it, and increasing his payment from 10,000 ducats to 16,500. This was a fitting tribute to one of the most able popes in history. Writing to his father, Lodovico, in February 1513, Michelangelo commented on the pledge made to him by Julius's heirs regarding the tomb: "It was promised me that in a few days it would be arranged and I would begin work."

Although the promised contract was not signed until the following May, Michelangelo nevertheless threw himself into his work, finalizing his plans for the statues and concentrating on the architectural and sculptural ornamentation for the base of the tomb. Of the three statues completed between 1513 and 1516, only the colossal *Moses*, would remain a part of the project. (The other two figures, known as the *Slaves*, eventually found their way to the Louvre Museum in Paris.)

After he saw the *Moses* for the first time, an astonished Giorgio Vasari wrote, "One might almost believe that the chisel had become a brush." In the *Moses*, the power lies not in the sheer magnitude of the work but rather in the drama of its presence, the steadfast gaze of eyes that are both commanding and visionary. There is passion in the figure, massive and strong beneath the draped garment, power in

"One might almost believe that the chisel had become a brush."

According to Michelangelo's original design, the Moses *would be one of many spectacular carvings.*

the veined hands that clutch the tablets holding the Ten Commandments, turbulence in the torrent of beard that flows from cheek to waist

By contrast to the *Moses*, the two twisted figures known as the *Slaves* appear to have struggled to break free of their bondage. The bodies are twisted to the point of exhaustion and the serenity of their faces suggest quiet submission to overwhelming odds. Scholars believe that the *Slaves* represent the liberal arts, set free by Julius's faithful support.

In January 1518, after completing his selection of the Carrara marbles, Michelangelo returned to Rome to sign the contract for an expanded chapel facade which now included twenty-two statues. During the following month, however, Cardinal de Medici, acting for the new pope, Leo X, in matters of finance, ordered the sculptor to stop all marble shipments coming from Carrara and to open quarries that were within the territory of Florence. With this, a deeply discouraged Michelangelo asked that the contract be abandoned, and the capricious Medicis offered no resistance. The heavy cost of building the new St. Peter's was draining the papal treasury and rumors of another war were clouding the skies over Italy.

But the ambitious Leo enjoyed a lavish lifestyle and poured what was left of the Vatican finances into new titles and lands for his family and papal favorites. To pay for all this, the pontiff levied heavy taxes on the people, despite warnings from his cardinals.

Within a short time, resentment of the pope's demands increased amid reports that church officials in Germany were taking huge profits from funds being collected. Leo continued to ignore the trouble that was brewing, having already made little of the "monkish squabble" that resulted when a priest named Martin Luther nailed a list of Church abuses to the doors of a church in Wittenberg, Germany. The act would lead to a split in the Church.

In 1520, despite the religious and political problems facing the country, a whimsical Leo ordered Michelangelo to build a great tomb for the Medicis in the San Lorenzo Chapel in Florence. Eager to return home, the sculptor immediately went to work on the design, later heading back to Carrara (with the Medicis' permission) to begin the tedious job of selecting the marble.

After thirteen months on the Medici tomb assignment, the artist received word that Pope Leo X had died of pneumonia, leaving both the Church and the country reeling toward disaster. No sooner had the news arrived than the heirs of Julius II demanded that Michelangelo finish the former pope's tomb or forfeit all the money that had been paid him.

In 1523, Leo's successor, the elderly Adrian VI, died and was replaced by yet another Medici, the wily Cardinal Giulio, who took the name of Clement VII. For the moment, Michelangelo's troubles with Julius's heirs were over, and he was sent back to Florence to continue with the Medici tombs.

Michelangelo moved ahead with the project but was interrupted by a restless Pope Clement, who wanted him to drop what he was doing to design a Medici library. On another occasion, the pontiff demanded that statues of Leo and himself be added to the tomb collection. During this same period, the beleaguered sculptor heard fresh demands from the Julius heirs, who ordered the completion of the papal tomb.

In 1527, Rome was hit by tragedy when Clement VII—who had thrown his political support to the Spanish emperor Charles V with the defeat of the French two years before—switched sides again to form a "Holy League" aimed at driving the Spanish out of Italy permanently. Brutally retaliating, Spanish and German mercenaries marched on the city. Clement fled to Castel Sant'-Angelo, where he watched in horror as thousands were slaughtered and buildings and homes burned to the ground. Later, disguised as a beggar, the pope escaped with his life. But in the meantime, Rome had been sacked, and a once bountiful papal treasury had been emptied by the excessive spending of the Medicis.

When news of the disaster reached Florence,

*In addition to his sculpture projects for the Medicis,
Michelangelo designed this staircase leading
to the Medici library.*

the citizens seized their chance to drive the Medicis from power and restore the republic. Michelangelo halted his work on the Medici tombs and made further sketches for the Julius project. Meanwhile, the indecisive Pope Clement made still another incredible move, changing political sides again to win the support of Charles V, whose army he borrowed in an attempt to recapture Florence.

With this, the independent Florentines dug in their heels and prepared themselves for a siege. Michelangelo abandoned his art and moved into action, helping reinforce the defenses of the city walls.

On July 8, 1528, while the people of Florence were fortifying themselves against invasion, Michelangelo's beloved brother Buonarroto died, leaving a wife and two children. The sculptor was heartbroken. Turning inward in his grief, he wrote the following to his nephew:

> Lionardo: He [Buonarroto] was alone on earth in exalting virtues with his great virtue . . . now in heaven he will have many companions, since there is no one there but those who loved the virtues so I hope that, from up there, he will complete my [work] down here.

After Buonarroto's death, Michelangelo's growing pessimism and fears about the swift passage of time became increasingly evident, although friends and contemporaries had been aware of the artist's dark side since his early days in Rome. In 1510, while Michelangelo was working on the Sistine Chapel ceiling, the young Raphael painted a figure in his great Vatican fresco, the *School of Athens*, that was clearly Michelangelo in the guise of Heraclitus, the "gloomy philosopher."

On April 8, 1511, Michelangelo accepted the post of chief of fortifications for the republic of Florence. For several months he traveled to cities throughout the territory, gaining a reputation as a skilled military engineer, although he lacked formal training in the field. By the end of September, however, certain that he had made enemies both inside and outside the republic, Michelangelo panicked and fled to Venice. Branded a rebel by Clement VII, the artist was now a political exile.

For two months, Michelangelo remained in Venice, occupying himself with his poetry, corresponding with friends, and relieving the tensions of war by a bit of painting. By November, news reached Michelangelo that Florence could not hold out much longer. Fearful for his family and friends, he disguised himself and returned to Florence but went into hiding after learning that the pope had threatened retaliation against leaders of the revolt.

On August 12, 1530, the republic of Florence

collapsed, and the Medicis returned to power. Michelangelo was pardoned by a guileful Clement because he made the solemn pledge that he would refuse all contracts other than the Medicis until he had completed his work on the San Lorenzo tombs.

Grateful for the pardon and eager to return to the Medici chapel projects, Michelangelo planned to spend the next several years working on the statues for San Lorenzo and finishing his architectural design for the handsome wood-paneled Laurentian Library.

Originally, the chapel of San Lorenzo was to have had four tombs, two single ones for Giuliano de Medici and Lorenzo, the Duke of Urbino, and a double one commemorating Lorenzo the Magnificent and his brother Giuliano. Sometime in 1523 or the year after, Clement VII had insisted on the addition of two more carved tombs representing himself and Leo X. But after the collapse of Florence, the Medici family was too absorbed in the tumultuous politics of the time to pay attention to the chapel tombs.

Only the tombs of Giuliano, Duke of Nemours, and Lorenzo, Duke of Urbino were completed. Each tomb influenced the great baroque period of future years, and each is a superb blending of architectural and sculptural styles. At the foot of Giuliano's tomb lie the uniquely balanced figures of *Night* and *Day*. On Lorenzo's tomb are the reclining figures of *Dawn and Twilight*. In niches above the tombs, two seated statues representing an animated Giuliano and a contemplative Lorenzo appear in directly contrasting moods.

In November 1531, Michelangelo's father, the tempestuous Lodovico, died at age 87. For the second time in less than four years, the artist had lost a member of his family. Michelangelo was once again in acute mourning and anguished by the complexity of his relationship with his father. For nearly thirty years, he had supported his entire family and met their needs and demands. But with Lodovico in particular, there had been no recognition of his genius or his generosity. Yet he grieved, as excerpts from one of his most poignant poems attest:

> Although my heart was already so weighed
> down,
> I still believed that I could make my escape
> from
> my great pain through my tears and weep-
> ing . . . now
> I must separate the tears, pen, and speech
> for the
> son who died first from those for you who died
> later.
> One was brother to me, and you father of us
> both
> I'm bound to him by love, to you by duty I don't

Michelangelo portrayed Lorenzo de Medici as quiet and thoughtful.

know which pain grips or upsets me more.
Memory still paints my brother for me, but it
   sculpts
you within my heart and stains my face even
   more.

After trips to Rome to settle accounts with the family of Julius II, a deeply saddened Michelangelo returned to Florence to finish his work on the Medici Chapel. In addition to the tombs for Giuliano and Lorenzo, he carved an exquisite statue of a seated *Madonna and Child*, returning to a theme that continued to hold his imagination and reverence.

By the end of the summer of 1534, angered by a turn of events that had ushered in the reign of the despised Alessandro de Medici, Michelangelo completed his work in the San Lorenzo Chapel, turned a few final details over to his assistants and left Florence for the last time. The city he had loved since his childhood had changed and would never return to its former glory. The artistic and literary achievements of the past would live on forever, but the independent spirit that had elevated Florence to greatness had been betrayed by a new breed of Medicis. Florence, he knew, would never be the same again.

CHAPTER 9

THE LAST JUDGMENT

The night before he left Florence for the last time, Michelangelo bid farewell to his family and wrote a short note to a friend: "I leave tomorrow. . . . and I shall not come back here again, and I am letting you know that as long as I live I shall always be at your service."

The decision to leave had not been easily made. The Florentines, including the artist's family, had suffered greatly during the time of the siege and would continue to do so under the tyrannical Alessandro de Medici. Michelangelo was torn between his allegiances to his family and to his art. With a heavy heart he gathered his belongings and prepared for his departure.

Michelangelo arrived in Rome on September 23, 1534. Two days later, Pope Clement VII died, leaving behind a deeply divided church and a country ravaged by war. Clement's successor, eager to continue the papacy's patronage of literature and the arts, wasted no time in summoning Michelangelo to the Vatican. Paul III, acting on an idea that had first been proposed by Pope Clement, had a new commission for the artist. As "Chief Architect, Sculptor, and Painter of the Apostolic Palace" he was to paint a new fresco for the wall above the high altar in the Sistine Chapel.

Michelangelo appealed to the pope to allow him to complete his contract for the Julius tomb, but the request was denied. "I have had this desire for thirty years," the angry pontiff roared, "and now that I am Pope, do you think I shall not satisfy it? I shall tear up the contract!"

"I shall tear up the contract!"

After months of negotiations and delays designed to forestall the project, Michelangelo began preparing his sketches for the giant fresco. Acting in accordance with the pontiff's wish, his design depicted the second coming of Christ, who returns to earth to fulfill the biblical prophesy of the Last Judgment. The painting would cover a vast area measuring 43 × 47 feet and would portray more than 350 figures. It would be the master's crowning achievement for the chapel.

For an entire year, Michelangelo directed the

reconstruction of the altar wall, blocking up two windows and reinforcing the plaster surface. Fifteenth-century frescoes by Perugino and the artist himself were eliminated in the process, and the wall was slanted to minimize the accumulation of dust and smoke from candles.

Finally, in 1535 or 1536, 61-year-old Michelangelo mounted the seven levels of his scaffold to begin the work that Giorgio Vasari would describe expressing "all the emotions that mankind can experience."

With the *Last Judgment*, Michelangelo depicted a world turned upside down by the evils of earthly pleasures, as well as the final condemnation of the wicked, who are sentenced to everlasting damnation in hell. The *Last Judgment* reveals the inner torment of the artist himself, fearful of death and despairing of "unknown sins" that consumed his soul. "I live in sin," he wrote. "I live dying within myself."

"I live dying within myself."

Michelangelo's themes in the *Last Judgment* are clearly the problems that would trouble him for the remainder of his life: his own personal spiritual anguish, salvation, and damnation, and his fears of Christ's rejection of him. Twice, Michelangelo placed himself in the whirlpool of

In the Last Judgment, *Michelangelo painted hundreds
of figures awaiting the ruling of Christ.*

tortured figures depicted in the fresco—in the expression of a terrified sinner suffering the heat of the inferno, and again on the flayed skin of Saint Bartholomew, unmistakable with its distorted face and broken nose.

At the center of the enormous work is the figure of Christ, beardless and vengeful with arm raised in denunciation of a sinful world. Surrounding him are representations of familiar saints, the Virgin Mary, prophets, martyrs, and Christ's apostles. In dramatic contrast to earlier depictions of the final Judgment Day, in which figures and scenes were arranged in a static series of levels, one on top of another, Michelangelo's interpretation thrives on movement, as figures bend and twist in response to the turbulence and the violent emotions that engulf them.

In the churning, tortured figures caught between the forces of good and evil, the influence of Dante is clear. Michelangelo drew upon his lifelong attachment to the works of the great poet to create the intensity of the actions taking place in the *Last Judgment*. Michelangelo identified with Dante's deeply held religious and political beliefs and now, as an exile from the same city that had once banished the poet, he found further reason to view him as a kindred spirit.

The *Last Judgment* can be seen as Michelangelo's visual interpretation of Dante's *Divine Com-*

Christ stands in the center of the Last Judgment *and determines who will go to hell and who will be saved.*

edy, in which the poet described his spiritual journey through hell and purgatory, and his eventual arrival in paradise. With each stage of the journey, Michelangelo's own intense torment emerges, particularly in his rendering of Dante's fierce boatman, Charon, ferrying the souls of the damned across the River Styx and into the gaping mouth of hell.

In a characteristic break with the artistic traditions of the fourteenth and fifteenth centuries, Michelangelo's outsized figures in the *Last Judgment* are stripped of their clothing. With the exception of Christ, the Virgin Mary, and several others, most figures wear little or nothing. Angels lack wings, and saints have no halos. The artist's intentions were forthright enough in his reverence for the beauty of the human form. He viewed his people as they had come into the world—free of the trappings of a structured society. But much of the world felt otherwise. When the *Last Judgment* was unveiled, many were outraged at the nudity of biblical figures. They accused Michelangelo of obscenity, charging that the work "did not belong in a papal chapel, but in public baths or brothels."

"Let him make the world a suitable place and painting will soon follow suit."

Criticism of the nudity continued. Years later, when a newly elected Pope Paul IV ordered Michelangelo to "make it suitable," the artist sarcastically shot back, "Tell the Pope that this is a small matter and it can easily be made suitable.

Let him make the world a *suitable place* and painting will soon follow suit."

A year after Michelangelo's death, a high Church council decided that the figures in the *Last Judgment* had to be clothed. Daniele da Volterra, a former pupil of the artist, was summoned to begin work on the coverings. Although it is perhaps more legend than fact, the story goes that one day Volterra had difficulty mixing his paints to match the colors he had used the day before, especially with the shades of green that he had applied to a gown for Saint Catherine, prompting one person to suggest that "The spirit of Michelangelo came back and switched paint pots on him." The conscientious Volterra was thereafter dubbed "the breeches maker" for his trouble.

For all of his anguish while working on the *Last Judgment*, Michelangelo exhibited moments of spirited humor. In a scene from Dante's *Inferno*, Minos, a menacing figure of the classical underworld, "stands . . . horrible and snarling." In Michelangelo's version, Minos bore the face of Biagio da Cesena, the pope's master of ceremonies, who had infuriated him by sneaking into the chapel and criticizing the nudity in the fresco. Viewing the final work, an equally angered Biagio begged the pope to remove the bewhiskered, donkey-eared caricature. Obviously amused, Paul III replied that his authority did not extend to hell, so the matter was out of his jurisdiction.

Other figures in the *Last Judgment* are recognizable by their earthly symbols. John the Baptist is shown in his camel skin, Peter holds the keys to the gates of heaven, Andrew carries his cross, Simon the carpenter carries his saw, and Blaise has his wool-carder's comb. The courageous Catherine, beheaded after her torture on a spiked wheel, holds the instrument of her anguish.

As a Vatican art historian describes the drama of the fresco, the living Christ dominates the scene, his upraised arm symbolizing the "gravitational force . . . that moves violently up and down creating a heaving sea in which angels and the damned, demons and the resurrected, appear to bob. Caught in the movement are the elect—who rise to heaven along the left side—and the damned—falling down along the right side while vainly fighting the avenging angels. Below . . . out of the whirlpool . . . the dead, painfully . . . returning to life . . . [and] Charon and his boat . . . epitomize . . . all the despair of hell."

On October 31, 1541, following six years of labor and nearly three decades after the unveiling of the Sistine Chapel ceiling, the *Last Judgment* was finished. The first to view the masterpiece was Pope Paul III, who fell to his knees in prayer. Condivi wrote that Michelangelo "expressed all that the art of painting can do with the human figure." Vasari later commented, "The intention of this extraordinary man has been to refuse to paint anything but the human body in its best proportioned and most perfect forms . . . likewise the play of the passions and contentments of the soul." With the completion of the *Last Judgment*, Michelangelo raised Italian Renaissance painting to its ultimate level of expression, changing forever the course of figurative art. With it, he signaled a warning against the evils of earthly vanities and the irreversible finality of the Judgment Day—a signal as strong as any the fiery Savonarola had ever sent.

"Expressed all that the art of painting can do with the human figure."

When Michelangelo was working on the *Last Judgment*, he met the two people with whom he would form the closest relationships of his later years. Tommaso de' Cavalieri was a handsome, 23-year-old nobleman from a distinguished Roman family when he met the artist. Polished and well educated, he shared Michelangelo's need for intellectual growth, and they remained close friends until the master's final hour. Cavalieri and the artist wrote to each other, and Michelangelo dedicated a number of poems to him.

Vittoria Colonna was equally inspirational to the artist. The widow of Ferrante Francesco d'Avalos, the Marchese of Pescara, Vittoria Colonna was a gifted poet, and like Michelangelo, was deeply religious. Devoting much of her life and writings to spiritual subjects, the Marchesa "sought to raise her mind above earthly affairs and fix [it] on divine ones." Vittoria frequently removed herself to a convent where she spent her days in prayer and meditation. During these periods, she welcomed the artist's company, and the two would stroll through the gardens of San Silvestro a Monte Cavallo, a Dominican retreat. They spoke of their mutual concerns and his increasing religious piety. Michelangelo believed that his friend had done him a "great favor" by "bringing [him] back from death to life." Vittoria Colonna valued her tender friendship with the master, once telling him that, "In Rome those who know you esteem you more than your works; those who do not know you esteem the least part of you, even the work of your hands."

Michelangelo dedicated many of his poems to Vittoria. In one of his loveliest, he compares shaping a blank canvas or block of stone with his friend's ability to reshape him spiritually and offer him hope:

> If it's true, lady, that you,
> although divine in beauty, can still live
> like a mortal creature and eat and sleep
> and speak among us here then not to
> follow you—your grace and mercy having
> put an end to doubt [to your spiritual
>   goodness]
> what penalty fits such an outrageous sin?

In February 1547, Vittoria Colonna died, leaving a permanent void in the artist's life.

Serious illness struck the master on at least two occasions. With the passing of time, he grew increasingly aware of the infirmities that come with advanced age. Afflicted with physical problems that ranged from kidney stones to deafness in one ear, Michelangelo lashed out with black humor in a lengthy discourse of metaphors that mocked his "earthly burden":

> I've got a bumblebee inside my jug [ear]
> some bones and strings inside my leather bag
> [bones and sinew inside the skin]
> and three pills of pitch inside my little vial
> [kidney stones]

. . . teeth like the keys on a wind instrument
at whose movements my voice may sound
or cease. . .
My face has a shape that's enough to terrify,
My clothes could chase crows, with no further
  rags.

Despite Michelangelo's deepening frustration
about work that he had not yet accomplished,
there were a number of high points during these
years. He had at last come to an agreement with
the heirs of Julius II and had installed a smaller
version of the Julius tomb. He had begun his last
exquisite frescoes, the *Conversion of Saint Paul*
and the *Crucifixion of Saint Peter* for the Pauline
Chapel, and had made preliminary sketches for
the redesigning of the Farnese Palace, the hered-
itary home of Pope Paul III's family. He also found
time to design the magnificent square on Capito-
line Hill, among other works commissioned for
the rebuilding of Rome.

Now past seventy years in age, Michelangelo
was appointed chief architect of the new St.
Peter's Basilica, the massive domed cathedral in
the heart of Vatican City. For the next seventeen
years, the artist occupied his days with plans for
this majestic project, giving freely of his genius "to
the glory of God, in honor of Saint Peter and for
the salvation of my soul." He was thoroughly

devoted to the Basilica project, saying, "I am old, and can leave nothing more of myself . . . and I do this service for God, and in Him I place all my hope." Embittered and angered by the tumultuous times in which he lived, Michelangelo would paint no more, and his writing and sculpture would concentrate on spiritual subjects, such as a new *Pietà*, which he began in 1547 for the adornment of his own tomb.

Between 1548 and 1555, Michelangelo suffered the death of two more family members, his brothers Giovansimone and Gismondo. He also witnessed the deaths of three popes, Paul III, Julius III, and Marcellus II. The most crushing blow came with the loss of his devoted servant, Urbino.

Michelangelo grieved for these losses, wondering if his death, too, was coming soon. Little did he know that one of his greatest achievements, the final design for the great *dome* of St. Peter's Basilica, lay ahead.

CHAPTER 10

ARCHITECT OF ST. PETER'S BASILICA

The great Basilica of St. Peter's was already more than one thousand years old when Michelangelo was appointed chief architect for the new design. Commissioned by Emperor Constantine soon after the Edict of Milan guaranteed freedom of worship to all Christians, it was consecrated in A.D. 326. A recent convert to the new religion, Constantine himself completed an act of penitence by ceremonially carrying twelve baskets of earth, one by one, on his back.

Built to represent the center of all Christendom, the original church was shaped like a Roman basilica—a long, empty hall decorated with frescoes of the earliest popes and scenes from the Bible. At the far end of the hall stood Saint Peter's funeral monument, on top of which was the papal altar, rebuilt by Pope Sixtus IV in the year of Michelangelo's birth. Over the saint's tomb was an *arch* inscribed—with no little modesty—

with Constantine's words: "As it was with Your guiding hand that he exalted the world to the heavens by his triumph, Constantine the victor built this house for You."

Over the centuries, many side chapels, gothic windows, and more than one hundred new altars were added to the basilica, which was the largest church in the world. Later on, the church was further enhanced with statues of saints, gilded furnishings, silk wall hangings, and oriental tapestries. During the Middle Ages, the most revered treasure was the purported bones of Saint Peter (which were excavated in 1953 and declared authentic in 1968 by Pope Paul VI after extensive study by anthropologists, chemists, and other specialists). Other sacred relics became part of the Vatican collection, including the bones of Andrew the Apostle, Peter's brother.

Remarkably, for 1,200 years, the old basilica had survived numerous attacks by both outside invaders and and rival factions among the Italian nobility. But it was Julius II who insisted that the ancient building be torn down and replaced with a light, spacious, and elegant church that would be the spiritual glorification of the Renaissance. Ironically, the funds needed to fulfill Julius's dream, which was supposed to represent the unity of worldwide faith, became the ultimate reason for the greatest schism in the Church's history.

Julius's first architect for the new basilica,

Donato Bramante, lacked the funds needed to begin construction and proceeded to plunder Rome's greatest antiquity—the Roman Forum. Mercilessly destroying the old basilica, he gained the nickname *Mastro Ruinante*, "Master Ruiner."

Bramante's design called for a church in the shape of a Greek cross with a cupola, or dome, atop the intersection of the two arms, resembling the dome of another famous building in Rome— the Pantheon. By the time he died in 1514, only four huge pilasters, or rectangular columns, had been built—again, due to a shortage of funds. Bramante was succeeded by three artists working as a team—Raphael, Giuliano da Sangallo, and Fra Giocondo. This group was followed by Michelangelo's friend Antonio da Sangallo, whose wooden model greatly changed Bramamte's original design, which Michelangelo referred to as "clear, pure, light and isolated all around." Michelangelo accused the entire Sangallo family—"the sect," as he called them—of having "deviated from the truth," squandering public funds, and wasting valuable time. Construction on the building crept along at a snail's pace. Weeds sprouted on the new walls amid ruins of the old church that had been left standing in order for worship to continue.

The project was at a virtual standstill when Michelangelo took over as chief architect in Januuary 1547, following Sangallo's death. Despite their friendship and his criticism of Sangallo's work, Michelangelo resisted the appointment when it came. Toward the end of his life, he declared, "It was not of my will that I built Saint Peter's, and I have always rendered [this] service not only gratis but at great pain and personal discomfort."

To the shock and dismay of the project's donors and administrators, Michelangelo's revised master plan called for demolishing almost everything Sangallo had accomplished and reducing the design slightly—"diminishing its size but increasing its greatness," as Vasari reported. Returning to Bramante's original draft, Michelangelo incorporated the idea of a central structure—the Greek cross—topped by a cupola and four smaller cupolas over the corner chapels. Pope Paul III gave written assurance that the master's entire design would proceed without alteration after his death. Michelangelo's supreme achievement for St. Peter's Basilica was the monumental dome, which he fashioned after Filippo Brunelleschi's dome for the cathedral of Florence. Asked to create a dome of splendor for the basilica that would surpass Brunelleschi's in

"Diminishing its size but increasing its greatness."

St. Peter's Dome stands today as testimony to Michelangelo's genius for architecture.

magnificence, Michelangelo replied that it would be "larger, yes but not more beautiful."

During the last four years of his life, Michelangelo's health deteriorated to the point where he had difficulty walking to the construction site of St. Peter's Basilica. Yet he continued to do so while working on his final sculptural projects, the *Pietà* and the *Deposition*, a work he carved for his own tomb.

He had grown quite frail. He was deaf in one ear and plagued by kidney stones, which caused him great pain. His eyes were dimmed by years of toil on the Sistine ceiling, after which he had found it necessary to hold his correspondence above his head in order to read them. He was no longer able to communicate by letter with what friends remained living, and he no longer had any wish to express his most private thoughts in poetry. "I have reached," he wrote to his biographer and faithful friend Giorgio Vasari, "the twenty-fourth hour of my day, and . . . no project arises in my brain which hath not the figure of death graven upon it."

The old man slept little now. In the darkest hours of the night, he continued work on his final *Pietà*, his hands trembling as they guided hammer and chisel by the light of a candle. Hours passed as the sculptor chipped away, brushing the dust of the marble tenderly from the slumping figure of the dead Christ.

*Michelangelo spent his last days carving
yet another* Pietà.

For three-quarters of a century, Michelangelo's art had been his inspiration and his demon. The mighty had fallen to their knees in worship and reverence for his achievements. He had turned his wealth over to the well-being of his selfish family, and he had fought the good fight for his beloved "country," Florence. He had won the fame he so urgently longed for and the respect and envy of his contemporaries. Yet he was alone.

The final moments came on Monday, February 18, 1564, less than a month before his ninetieth birthday. News of his illness traveled quickly. At his bedside were two of his most devoted friends, Daniele da Volterra and Tommaso Cavalieri.

"O Daniello, io sono spacciato, mi ti raccomando, non mi abbandonare,... Oh, Daniello, I'm finished, I beg you, don't leave me."

After his death, the hierarchy of Rome, wanting to claim him as their own, planned to bury the master in their own city. But an equally determined Lionardo, the master's long-suffering nephew, stole Michelangelo's body and sent it off to Florence disguised as his goods.

There, in the city that he had so passionately loved, he was laid to rest in Santa Croce, the church of his ancestors. Vasari, his biographer and loyal friend, carved his magnificent tomb and the distinguished Benedetto Varchi delivered his eulogy, a two-hour epic that "paid homage to the master's unprecedented achievements in all three visual arts and poetry."

After the master's funeral, an inventory of his lovely home on the Macel de'Corvi, a residence "of several stories, with reception rooms, bedrooms, grounds, and a vegetable garden," included a sealed box with some 8,000 crowns, 10 drawings, and 3 statues, including the *Pietà*.

Construction on the Basilica of Saint Peter's continued, with stops and starts, for the next sixty-two years until its consecration on November 18, 1626. The final masterpiece housed the blessed *Pietà* of Michelangelo's youth. And it was there that the spirit of the master would abide. He had left his "earthly prison" with works and plans unfulfilled, but the magnificence of his achievements would last for an eternity. On his deathbed, Michelangelo had confided to his two devoted friends, "I regret that I have not done enough for the salvation of my soul and that I am dying just as I am beginning to learn the alphabet of my profession."

The light is extinguished.

A NOTE ON SOURCES

A wide variety of sources assisted me in the writing of *Michelangelo: Genius of the Renaissance.* Among these, the following works will be helpful to young readers and students in gathering materials for essays and reports: Vincent Cronin's *Florence of the Medici* (The Story of Man Books, National Geographic, 1977); John J. Putnam's *Michelangelo's Rome* (The Story of Man Books, National Geographic, 1997); and Meg Nottingham Walsh's article in *National Geographic*, May, 1994: "Out of the Darkness, Michelangelo's Last Judgment." Readers interested in the poetry and letters of Michelangelo, as well as an excellent biographical sketch, chronology, and further references and notes, should see Gilbert Creighton and Robert Linscott's *Complete Poems and Selected Letters of Michelangelo* (Princeton University Press, 1980). Valerio Mariani's *Michelangelo the*

Painter, written in celebration of the 400th anniversary of the artist's death in 1564, is noteworthy for its fine collection of sketches and color plates. Two additional poetry collections with background sketches that proved helpful in gaining further glimpses into the private thoughts, inspirations, and frustrations of the artist are Sidney Alexander's *The Complete Poetry of Michelangelo* (Ohio University Press, 1991) and Elizabeth Jennings's *The Sonnets of Michelangelo* (Doubleday, 1970).

The recent, extensive restorations to the Sistine Chapel have been reproduced in two beautiful volumes. *Michelangelo the Last Judgment: A Glorious Restoration* (Harry N. Abrams, 1997) contains a number of magnificent color reproductions of the fresco. Robin Richmond's *Michelangelo and the Creation of the Sistine Chapel* (Crescent Books, 1995) offers a full-color foldout of the restored ceiling.

FOR MORE INFORMATION

BOOKS

Cairns, Trevor. *Renaissance and Reformation.* New York: Cambridge University Press, 1987.

Coughlin, Robert. *The World of Michelangelo.* New York: Time-Life Books, 1966.

Grazione, Antonio, Fabrizio Macinelli & Francesco Rossi. *Michelangelo and Raphael in the Vatican.* Rome: Vatican Museum, 1989.

Green, Jen. *Michelangelo.* New York: Barrons Juveniles, 1994.

INTERNET RESOURCES

Michelangelo
http://sunsite.unc.edu/cjackson/michelan/
In addition to a general background of Michelan-

gelo's life, this site provides easy access to photos of the artist's sculpture and frescoes.

Michelangelo Buonarroti
http://www.michelangelo.com/buonarroti.
html
This site provides biographical information on the famous artist and links to illustrations of his greatest masterpieces.

Sistine Chapel
http://www.christusrex.org/www1/sistine/
0-Tour.html
The homesite of the Sistine Chapel provides illustrations and maps of the ceiling.

The Uffizi Gallery
http://www.televisual.net/uffizi/index.html
This is the homesite of the world-famous museum Uffizi in Florence. It provides links to rooms in the museum, allowing you to enjoy the works of Michelangelo and other Renaissance artists.

arch a curved structure that helps support a building or bridge

barrel vault a rounded ceiling or roof

basilica early Christian church, rectangular in shape

bas-relief figure carved or cast in such a way that it is raised from its background

dome roof shaped like half of a sphere

fresco painting made on a wall or ceiling while the plaster is still wet

mosaic a picture or pattern made of small pieces of stone, glass, or tile

mural painting, usually of a large scene, on a wall

pietà word meaning "pity" or "compassion"; a representation of the Virgin Mary holding the body of Christ

renaissance a rebirth of learning and culture

CHRONOLOGY

1475	Michelangelo was born on March 6 in the village of Caprese, Tuscany.
1481	Mother dies.
1488	Leaves school and becomes apprenticed to painter Domenico Ghirlandaio.
1489	Leaves Ghirlandaio's studio to study sculpture at San Marco gardens.
1492	Lorenzo the Magnificent (de Medici) dies.
1495	Carves the *Cupid*.
1496	Carves the *Bacchus* while in Rome.
1497	Travels to Carrera to select marble.
1498	Returns to Rome and is commissioned to carve the *Pietà*.
1501	Commissioned to carve the *David*.
1503	Commissioned to carve the Twelve Apostles.
1504	Commissioned to paint the *Battle of Cascina* fresco.

1505	Ordered by Julius II to begin a tomb requiring forty statues.
1506	Quarrels with Julius and is finally pardoned. Begins work on colossal bronze statue of the pope.
1508	Begins work on the Sistine Chapel.
1512	Completes the Sistine Chapel.
1513	Julius II dies. New contract with Julius's heirs. Works on *Moses* and the slaves.
1516	Makes models of Medici chapel.
1520	Contract for Medici chapel canceled. Begins work on Medici tombs.
1522–23	Works on Medici tombs.
1523	Agrees to work on Medici Library.
1529	Becomes chief of fortifications for Florence.
1530	Returns to work on Medici tombs.
1531	Father dies.
1534	Begins work on the *Last Judgment.*
1541	*Last Judgment* is completed.
1542	Finishes the *Moses.*
1545	Julius II tomb is installed.
1547	Appointed architect of St. Peter's Basilica.
1556–64	Continues supervision of construction of St. Peter's.
1564	Dies while working on a *Pietà* for himself.

INDEX

ABOUT THE AUTHOR

Jayne Pettit has written numerous books for young people, including *Maya Angelou: Journey of the Heart* (Lodestar/Dutton, 1996), *A Time to Fight Back* (Macmillan, 1995 and Houghton Mifflin, 1996), and *A Place to Hide: True Stories of the Holocaust* (Scholastic, 1993, Macmillan, 1994), which has sold close to 140,000 copies since its publication in the United States and Britain. Her next book for Franklin Watts/Grolier, *Jane Goodall's Wonderful World of the Chimpanzees,* will be available in spring 1999.